True Prayers
HEAR HIM SPEAK

*177 Powerful Prayers to Help You Heal
Through the Power of God's Word*

by Lacey Whittaker

Edited by Lil Barcaski and Linda Hinkle

Published by: GWN Publishing
www.GWNPublishing.com

Cover Design: Kristina Conatser Captured by KC Design

ISBN: 979-8-9859746-1-4

DEDICATION

I am dedicating this book to my precious Auntie Rita. She lived it through and through and most of these prayers came from a place in her life that we all walked through together. I love you more than you even know. Thank you for being a spiritual mother like no other.

I want to thank my ever-loving Jesus Team; without you this couldn't be possible.

INTRODUCTION

In this book you will find 177 True Prayers. This is a continuation of True Prayers book 1. Just diving in deeper. You will read about the struggles we all face, battling sickness, anxiety, and fears.

Maybe you struggle with un-forgiveness and hurt. These prayers will help you surrender all that life throws at you and find hope in our loving, forgiving Father who desires to guide and provide, give us peace and joy, healing and power to live here in this world.

1

I praise you for your goodness. I praise you for your strength. I praise you mighty God, for all you have shown me. I praise you for your love and glory. I praise you for your son's story. I praise you. May I never miss a second to praise the one that gives me each day sealed with a kiss.

> "I will praise You, O Lord my God, with all my heart,
> and I will glorify Your name forevermore."
> –Psalm 86:12 *NKJV*

2

Lord, when family and friends try to come and cut me down, when jealousy seems like it's all around, when all I pray and all I do is want to honor and glorify truth, when they say I'm false and not lined up, when they knock me down and I get back up, help me forgive, for they do not know what they do. Help me forgive just like you.

> "Be kind and helpful to one another, tender-hearted [compassionate, understanding], forgiving one another [readily and freely], just as God in Christ also forgave you."
>
> –Ephesians 4:32 *AMP*

3

When our world seems to fall apart and we feel so alone, when the pressure to measure up is not from your throne, when others label and kick you down, help me remember, you won that round. Help me to have eyes to see when others persecute me. Help me to repent and not to speak.

> *"Let Your hand be ready to help me,*
> *For I have chosen Your precepts."*
>
> —Psalms 119:173 *AMP*

4

Lord, you came for the broken. You came for the lost. You came to save me at the worst cost. You sent your son so I may have life. You are my true heart's delight. Help me remember what you went through. Help me to shake the lesser things and glorify truth. Help me to see it's only you. Help me release so I can be free in your everlasting peace and receive fully what you died to give me.

"... who purchased our freedom and forgave our sins."
–Colossians 1:14 *NLT*

Lord, help me to be kind. Help me to die daily to my flesh. It's a raring ugly beast, full of many insecurities. Help me to be kind. Help me to cast out my mind and follow what you have put in my heart. Kindness shows love and it's a start.

> "So, as God's own chosen people, who are holy [set apart, sanctified for His purpose] and well-beloved [by God Himself], put on a heart of compassion, kindness, humility, gentleness, and patience [which has the power to endure whatever injustice or unpleasantness comes,
> with good temper];"
>
> —Colossians 3:12 *AMP*

6

Lord, help me keep it simple. I know you did not form us to bear so much. Help me let go and pour from your cup. Help me stay simple. I know simple will bring me peace and that fruit is everything to me.

> "The law of the Lord is perfect [flawless], restoring and refreshing the soul; the statutes of the Lord are reliable and trustworthy, making wise the simple."
>
> —Psalms 19:7 *AMP*

7

Peace comes after obedience. Help me, Lord, for when I may stray, help me get back to your ways. I know peace will come and stay, only when I choose to obey.

> "So, beloved, since you are looking forward to these things, be diligent and make every effort to be found by Him [at His return] spotless and blameless, in peace [that is, inwardly calm with a sense of spiritual well-being and confidence, having lived a life of obedience to Him]."
>
> −2 Peter 3:14 *AMP*

8

I will take my thoughts captive. Make them obey your word, your truth. Release my enemies. I give them to you. Release my cares, insecurities, too. I will lay them at your feet. Let go and live again. Be free in you, that's all my heart knows to do.

"For the word of God is alive and powerful. It is sharper than the sharpest two-edged sword, cutting between soul and spirit, between joint and marrow. It exposes our innermost thoughts and desires."

—Hebrews 4:12 *NLT*

Keep letting go of the discomfort and pain. Let it all go in Jesus' name. Let it go now. Watch all those troubles. Bow down to the King of Kings, be filled with his glory. Now go in peace and we shall trust you, Lord with everything.

> *"Don't worry or surrender to your fear. For you've believed in God, now trust and believe in me also."*
>
> —John 14:1 *TPT*

10

Victory is priceless like a gold gem in the desert, a rock, a precious stone in a waterfall of truth. My God, I adore and honor you. Help me break away from my past. You have made me a new creation at last.

> "For you have acquired new creation [in] life which is continually being renewed into the likeness of the One who created you; giving you the full revelation of God."
>
> –Colossians 3:10 TPT

Holy, Holy, Holy. Are you Holy, Holy, Holy and true? Are you that died for me? To save and set me free. Holy, Holy, Holy. Are you Holy, Holy, Holy? I see. I believe. I dream. Holy, I keep.

> *"For Scripture says: 'You are to be holy, because I am holy.'"*
>
> —1 Peter 1:16 *TPT*

12

You are the way, the truth, the life. You are alpha and omega, the prince of peace. My eyes cannot see all the glory you behold. This is the story that shall be told.

> "For you are King-God, the Most High God over all the earth. You are exalted above every supernatural power!"
>
> —Psalms 97:9 *TPT*

All who are lost, be found. Yield to the Holy Spirit. Take this gift given and run. Be undone. Go now. Forgive. Let go. Live in peace. Live free from other's insecurities. When they try to come and take you with a knife, fight back, without pride. Just be still, be still and he will. God will handle, he will.

> "Let the evildoers be at their worst and the morally filthy continue in their depravity—yet the righteous will still do what is right, and the holy will still be holy."
>
> —Revelation 22:11 *TPT*

14

I hear my father say, rest child, rest. Watch me, seek me with your everything. I have called you to rest and be blessed, so blessed by this rest. Rest your heart, mind, body and soul. Rest child and let go of your worries, self-doubt and past. Let go and simply ask of these things, ask and receive. Ask and receive. My loving kindness shall follow you all your days, now release, be free and sit. Soak it all in with me.

> *"Take My yoke upon you and learn from Me [following Me as My disciple], for I am gentle and humble in heart, and you will find rest [renewal, blessed quiet] for your souls."*
>
> –Matthew 11:29 *AMP*

Lord, help us to enjoy each day, each moment, each hour, each breath. We never know when you will call us home so, let us be in each moment and not look in the past nor the day ahead. Help us, lead us to be still and just be.

Be still in his presence.

16

How much longer do we walk through? How much longer? I need you. How much longer do we keep getting hit? How much longer? I can barely take another step. How much longer? I'm fighting for air. How much longer? All my cares seem to be just like a bad dream. How much longer? Lord, please tell me how much longer do I walk in this. How much longer can I take it? How much longer, Lord? I just need to know how much longer before all this blows. How much longer is something I ask but, Father, if it takes a lifetime before I see relief, I will serve you with all the best of me.

*"**Behold**, how happy and fortunate is the man whom God reproves, so do not despise or reject the discipline of the Almighty [subjecting you to trial and suffering]."*

—Job 5:17 *AMP*

Lord, where are you when I'm crying out? Where are you when I come to doubt? Where are you when I feel there is nothing left? Where are you? I hear you say, I have never left. Where are you and why am I feeling like this? Where are you? Can you come and take this? Where are you? I don't understand. I hear you say, this is all part of my plan. Where are you when loved ones die? Where are you when children are hurt? Where are you? How can I move past this hurt? I hear you say, child, oh child, I have never left. Let me tell you about my death. What I gave for you to live, what I gave to love you until the end. What I gave for heaven. You will see what I gave was faith to believe.

> *"This is my command—be strong and courageous!*
> *Do not be afraid or discouraged. For the*
> *Lord your God is with you wherever you go."*
>
> –Joshua 1:9 *NLT*

18

Prayers are like heavens' cares wrapped up and thrown deep into a pillar of belief. You hold them all, and this I shall keep, the comfort I shall reap.

"Your promise revives me; it comforts me in all my troubles."

—Psalms 119:50 *NLT*

Precious, sovereign king, you have given me everything. You hold it all in your hands, you give it all according to your plan. Riches, love, honor and grace, oh how I love to see your face shine upon my darkest days. Awaken me, help me to seek and pray.

> *"I will answer them before they even call to me. While they are still talking about their needs, I will go ahead and answer their prayers!"*
>
> —Isaiah 65:24 *NLT*

20

You have called the sick and dead to rise, you have called us to sacrifice. You have called the orphans and widows too. You have called us to love and adore you. You have called us to rise above, you have called us to shine like the morning sun. You have called us to obey and know truth, you have called us. Father, let us honor and love you.

> "And because we are his children, God has sent the Spirit of his Son into our hearts, prompting us to call out, 'Abba, Father.'"
>
> —Galatians 4:6 *NLT*

Live and never die, let me hear your hearts cry for mine. I shall weep to hear you in pain, to see you in my darkest day. Hold on to me, hold on. I have given you breath, oh breathe. Child, I will be back soon in the hardest days you have faced. Remember I will be there every second of the way. This life will be no longer. Soon, I will take you home to be with me forever in eternity.

> *"From eternity to eternity I am God. No one can snatch anyone out of my hand. No one can undo what I have done."*
>
> –Isaiah 43:13 *NLT*

We cast worry, anxiety and depression. All these things are games the enemy loves to play. Oh, how he loves bondage, too, but I love to rebuke and say to you, Father, Jesus, Holy Spirit, you are true, never will I bow down to what is thrown not from you.

> "Pour out all your worries and stress upon him and leave them there, for he always tenderly cares for you."
>
> —1 Peter 5:7 *TPT*

You have called us up, you have called us out, you have called us to be about the one that has been made in the image of you, the one that proclaims so much truth. Father, today I bow and give my life again to you somehow, again and again you always forgive, and for this I'm chosen, and heaven sent.

> "Help me turn my eyes away from illusions so that I pursue only that which is true; drench my soul with life as
> I walk in your paths."
>
> –Psalms 119:37 *TPT*

24

Father, I come again, I lay down my burdens and repent. I put them down and leave them all there, Father, you are the one that holds these cares. I give them to you, Father. You say, look up, child, and speak truth, you may get knocked down, but rise again. You will prove I am the one honoring and protecting you.

> "Blessed [forgiven, refreshed by God's grace] are those who mourn [over their sins and repent], for they will be comforted [when the burden of sin is lifted]."
>
> —Matthew 5:4 *AMP*

The battle is won. I say, the battle is won. The battle is won. Get up, go fight and win. It's won, it's won, now go and grin, let no defeat take you to your knees, the Lord is fighting for you and for me.

The battle is won.

26

When I'm tired and feel like giving up, help me to lift my head up. When others come and mock me to get to you, help me forgive so I will not lose. When I feel like leaving and want to quit, help me to go forth and live and repent. Father, help me to stay in your will and never leave because I feel ill.

> "Cast your burden on the Lord [release it] and He will sustain and uphold you; He will never allow the righteous to be shaken (slip, fall, fail)."
>
> —Psalms 55:22 *AMP*

Father, I know you won't give any more than I can take, help me to see with eyes of faith, help me to prosper and grow in truth. Help me to never stop seeing you. Father, when hard times come again, help me remember you went through all of them. Father, when I feel like I can't take anymore, Father, come and hold me forever more.

> *"O God, do not be far from me;*
> *O my God, come quickly to help me!"*
>
> —Psalms 71:12 *AMP*

28

The enemy, the enemy loves to taunt and bluff. He loves to come and throw a punch. He loves to come and make me feel defeat, he loves to come and steal my peace. The enemy has no hold, no hold on me, I have Jesus and that's all I need.

> "The Lord will cause the enemies who rise up against you to be defeated before you; they will come out against you one way but flee before you seven ways."
>
> –Deuteronomy 28:7 *AMP*

Defeat, defeat, defeat, I hear the enemy say, but all I know to do is pray, pray, pray. You can't have my faith; I will rise and see another day. When the fight seems hard, when the day seems long, I know I have a helper to help me along. I cast you out and you must flee, my father is the prince of peace.

"Arise, O Lord, confront him, cast him down; save my soul from the wicked with Your sword."

–Psalms 17:13 *AMP*

30

When I struggle, when I fall, when I let too many fill my heart with their bark, help me to surrender. Help me to see, pull me back close so I can breathe. Help me get to the heart of the matter only to see that you, Father, always have only the best for me.

> *"I have told you all this so that you may have peace in me. Here on earth, you will have many trials and sorrows. But take heart, because I have overcome the world."*
>
> –John 16:33 *NLT*

You are not a dart. Set your guard, set your heart, don't let others throw you into a pit. Step up, you are not bound by men. You are known, you are loved, you are guided from your Father above.

"Guard your heart above all else, for it determines the course of your life."

–Proverbs 4:23 *NLT*

32

Lord, help me forgive, help me let go, help me to see, once that was isn't always what is forever to be. When others leave, when others curse, when others choose another course, help me see it's your plan for me. Help me forgive and live to be exactly what you have made me to fully be, even if I walk this alone, even if everyone leaves. At the end of the day, if it's just you and me, I will be alright, I will be just fine, I will always be able to dream and fly with you by my side.

> "Jesus replied, 'The Scriptures say, 'You must worship the Lord your God and serve only him.'"
>
> –Luke 4:8 *NLT*

Come behold the king, the king that plants your dreams. Let go of the rest, come to the one that gives your best. Lay your troubles, lay your cares, seek him now in your prayers.

> *"But when you pray, go into your most private room, close the door and pray to your Father who is in secret, and your Father who sees [what is done] in secret will reward you."*
>
> –Matthew 6:6 *AMP*

34

Why do people come against so harsh? Why do they call themselves followers but live in the dark? Where does this rage come from? What makes them come so completely undone? Where is the love? God, I cannot see, they say they honor you, but they disrespect me. Help me let go and lead by truth, help me let go and love them like you do.

> *"How can you say to your brother, 'Brother, allow me to take out the speck that is in your eye,' when you yourself do not see the log that is in your own eye? You hypocrite [play actor, pretender], first take the log out of your own eye, and then you will see clearly to take out the speck that is in your brother's eye.'"*
>
> –Luke 6:42 *AMP*

Lord, help me, I'm falling and cry out wondering where you went? Lord, help me to understand how this pain can be part of your plan. I follow you, I trust and obey, but long weeks like this, I feel so at bay. Never will you leave, never will I stray, help me Father, pull me up and show me how to pray.

"But she came and began to kneel down before Him, saying, 'Lord, help me!'"

–Matthew 15:25 *AMP*

36

Pain, agony, and sin tries to cut deep within; we are free from all of this, you died, you bled on that tree to save the lost like me. Father, help me never to take what you died and gave for us to live in abundant peace, for us to live so humble and free from all our insecurities.

> "We know that our old self [our human nature without the Holy Spirit] was nailed to the cross with Him, in order that our body of sin might be done away with, so that we would no longer be slaves to sin."
>
> —Romans 6:6 *AMP*

Father, help my restless heart and my weary soul, help me to let go of full control. Take me to a place where only I see your face, let me feel your grace and be healed from head to toe. Thank you for peace, strength, healing and dreams. Thank you for never leaving and always seeing, helping me push past and move on. Help me father to be so strong.

Amen

38

Let them scuttle in a huddle, let them worry and be afraid. Let them be, I will let them be. My Father sees, my Father sees. He has seen the worse of the worst and still agreed to be loving and kind. Forgiveness he holds, my Father knows when they scuttle and persecute you. They do it because of your honor to truth, your honor for him, so Father, if I am persecuted for you, let it be. I know what you took was greater than my eyes will ever see.

"So, I am well pleased with weaknesses, with insults, with distresses, with persecutions, and with difficulties, for the sake of Christ; for when I am weak [in human strength], then I am strong [truly able, truly powerful, truly drawing from God's strength]."

–2 Corinthians 12:10 *AMP*

Joy, oh joy, where does all this joy come from? Where does this joy come from? The fruit of peace has me. The fruit of joy I could not live without thee. Come joy, come. You have come on me like a flood. My heart is so happy I could sing your song of victory. This joy in my heart was yours from the start, oh this joy I have found, this joy is all around. My joy, my joy, my joy is everything, it is my victory.

> *"Always be full of joy in the Lord. I say it again—*
> *rejoice!"*
>
> –Philippians 4:4 *NLT*

40

Bruises, scars, lies, and bars, all this world holds, and some will never know this true relationship you could have when you let go and call upon his name. When you let go and say, Jesus, you died to save and I believe in you, Jesus, take my soul. I love and adore you.

"If you openly declare that Jesus is Lord and believe in your heart that God raised him from the dead, you will be saved."

–Romans 10:9 *NLT*

When I'm sick, when I'm in defeat, when prayers aren't answered quickly, when I cry, when I fear, Father, help me not see these cares. As I go to my knees, look up above, bow down to the Father of love, something changes. Something shifts because you, Father, only give life and life to the full healings, miracles and all goodness endured. Never shall I miss the timing. It's yours. I shall wait for the day you call us, and this world be no more.

"And God confirmed the message by giving signs and wonders and various miracles and gifts of the Holy Spirit whenever he chose."

—Hebrews 2:4 *NLT*

42

This life I live. I have had to choose more times than ten to let go, surrender, turn away from sin. To look up, walk forward in truth and win. It's not always easy I would say, but always worth it at the end of the day. As I lie and say Lord, Jesus, your will is my everything, my peace and comfort remains as I obey.

> *"Do not be wise in your own eyes; Fear the Lord*
> *[with reverent awe and obedience] and*
> *turn [entirely] away from evil."*
> —Proverbs 3:7 *AMP*

Hard times come. The enemy knocks sometimes. He stays even when the door is locked. I shut him out. I cast him down. I tell him this child doesn't mess around. Then I get weary and worn down. He thinks he won until the next round. The fight is over. It has been won. My father, my King, speaks over me. Child, go now and have peace.

> "Love bears all things [regardless of what comes],
> believes all things [looking for the best in each one],
> hopes all things [remaining steadfast during difficult
> times], endures all things [without weakening]."
> —1 Corinthians 13:7 AMP

44

The great, I am. You speak. The great, I am. I reap. The great, I am. Is everything. The great, I am is in you and me. The great, I am so holy and pure. The great, I am so mighty and sure. The great, I am the only one to know. The great, I am. I seek you and behold your kingdom is here to see your kingdom you left for me. Your kingdom is the greatest of these. Your kingdom forever I shall reap.

"God said to Moses, "I AM WHO I AM"; and He said, "You shall say this to the Israelites, 'I AM has sent me to you.'"

–Exodus 3:14 *AMP*

Holy Spirit, you come on and flood through my bones. You come so strong and this I know. It's you, you. I seek the wisdom and peace. Never shall you leave. I will always praise your name, Jesus, for sending Thee, the helper of many things. Oh, I could not imagine life without the Holy Spirit. You are so very true.

"May the God of hope fill you with all joy and peace in believing [through the experience of your faith] that by the power of the Holy Spirit you will abound in hope and overflow with confidence in His promises."

–Romans 15:13 *AMP*

46

Jesus, you cast our cares. Jesus, you are everywhere. In the darkest of days, you are the light in my face. Jesus, you are king. Jesus, you are truth. You are the bread that comes from above, you are everything in love. You, Jesus, will never miss the opportunity to stop and show us. Your kingdom come your will be done. Jesus, you are the Father's chosen son.

> *"Whoever confesses and acknowledges that Jesus is the Son of God, God abides in him, and he in God."*
>
> –1 John 4:15 *AMP*

47

All this world could go and not see. All this world looks past your victory. All this world, oh, how could they miss? How could they miss this precious gift that was sent to save us from hell, to save us and love us even when we fail. Oh, how could this world go a lifetime and not see, you came down and showed us your everlasting love and glory.

> *"Show us Your loving kindness, O Lord, and grant us Your salvation."*
>
> —Psalms 85:7 *AMP*

48

You sow and reap. Sow and reap. Father, all this what I sow and reap. All these seeds. Remember you sow even the bad, you may speak. So, Father, when I sow, help me see how I would like to reap from thee. Father, open my eyes. Help me see, for what I sow, I certainly shall see.

> "Now [remember] this: he who sows sparingly will also reap sparingly, and he who sows generously [that blessings may come to others] will also reap generously [and be blessed]."
>
> –2 Corinthians 9:6 *AMP*

I love to see where you take me. I love to let go and do your will. I love to not look for the bad in the dark places, but the growth that sprouts from being still. I love to look back and say, oh, that's what happens when I obey. Nothing in this world is better than following you, nothing, it's true.

> "Immediately they left their nets and followed Him [becoming His disciples, believing and trusting in Him and following His example]."
>
> —Matthew 4:20 *AMP*

50

Letting go of pride. Letting go of offense. You say we are chosen, and heaven sent. What else shall we fear? What else shall get us down? When you are the one that always turns it around, may we always stop and look for you. May we always stop and see the truth. Forgive and always forget, Father, you have called us to be heaven sent.

> "Whenever you stand praying, if you have anything against anyone, forgive him [drop the issue, let it go], so that your Father who is in heaven will also forgive you your transgressions and wrongdoings [against Him and others]."
>
> —Mark 11:25 *AMP*

Father, I look and do not see. I look and seek you on my knees, for I do not know what this world holds. I do not know. Oh, I do not know. For you have called and foretold, I hold onto truth. I hold onto you no matter what we go through. I will always see the best because of you.

> *"You judge according to human standards [just by what you see]. I do not judge anyone."*
>
> –John 8:15 *AMP*

52

Father, I pray everyone seeks your face. I pray, oh, how I pray, for one day everyone will see. Everyone will believe it's only you, that gave up everything to give us life and not death, to give us our very last breath. May we all seek you and see you are the one that holds the key to where we truly belong.

> *"Let us test and examine our ways and*
> *let us return to the Lord."*
>
> –Lamentations 3:40 *AMP*

I rebuke Satan. I rebuke his schemes. I rebuke the grip he tries to hold on me. I rebuke his pride and arrogance, too. I rebuke him now and will forever see you.

"And the Lord said to Satan, 'The Lord rebuke you, Satan! Even the Lord, who [now and ever] has chosen Jerusalem, rebuke you! Is this not a log snatched and rescued from the fire?'"

—Zechariah 3:2 *AMP*

54

Wake up, soldiers. Awake from your sleep, your Father has called you to reap, reap, reap. You were made to conquer and win. The victory you hold comes from him. Awake soldier, you have been called. Awake soldier, go on and walk, walk now in the know. Walk now and show the king of kings came for you. Walk soldier and speak so true.

"Let us not grow weary or become discouraged in doing good, for at the proper time, we will reap, if we do not give in."

–Galatians 6:9 *AMP*

When we let go of control and be held, when we let go and tell his story not ours, you see there is a life abundant and full in victory. When we let go and let God shine through, when we let go of petty things too, when we let go of ourselves for him, he will show you life greater than all men.

> "Take hold of instruction; [actively seek it, grip it firmly and] do not let go. Guard her, for she is your life."
>
> —Proverbs 4:13 *AMP*

56

Faith takes courage, trust, obedience, too. Faith you are something I never want to lose, for without faith, this life would be a mess. Without faith, I would live in distress. Faith, you have taught me a thing or two. Faith is something we don't see but believe it's true.

Our faith pulls us through.

You are not a dart I say. You cannot be thrown for others to say. They try to throw darts to put you away, to put you in a place where the enemy lays. Wake up, chosen one, it's true, the only dart thrown should be pointed to you. A Father that loves at all times. A father that sees us shine, go forth and leave it be. My Father knows my worth and that's everything. Set your guard. Set your heart. Those darts are meant to tear you apart. Oh, but my Father. I hear him say I have you to hold, put those darts away.

> *"Flash lightning and scatter my enemies; Send out Your arrows and confuse and embarrass and frustrate them."*
>
> **–Psalms 144:6 *AMP***

58

Never doubt, child. Never doubt. I am all about taking you, about, about in a whole new way. About, how about never shall you stray. Don't doubt these things that try to come and take. Don't doubt that's his weapon against your clout. Don't doubt and be about all I have given you. Don't doubt. Oh, one day soon you will be here and doubt, worry and fear will all be tossed forever, and you will be where you belong my dear.

> *"And you shall know [without any doubt] that I am in the midst of Israel [to protect and bless you], And that I am the Lord your God, And there is no other; My people will never be put to shame."*
>
> **–Joel 2:27 AMP**

Thorns. Thorns. Thorns in your side. Thorns. Thorns. Thorns in your side. You take them all, take my pride. Thorns. Thorns. Thorns in your side. When I release and let go, I can fly.

"By His breath the heavens are cleared; His hand has pierced the [swiftly] fleeing serpent."

–Job 26:13 *AMP*

60

Pruning. Pruning. Pruning is what you do to bear, to bear much juicy fruit. Pruning. Pruning. Pruning as hard as it can be, I know how wonderfully well it is for me prune. Prune this pride and insecurity. Prune. Prune. Prune it so I can leave it all lay at your feet. Soar above this fruit. I shall eat. Prune, oh, Father, prune. For my will is only to be used by you.

> "Every branch in Me that does not bear fruit, He takes away; and every branch that continues to bear fruit, He [repeatedly] prunes, so that it will bear more fruit [even richer and finer fruit]."
>
> —John 15:2 *AMP*

Satan. Satan. The tools you use. Satan, oh, Satan, how you love to beat up and use all your lies to hit between the eyes. All your snares to form our cares. We have won. Conquered. It's true your lies are worthless and so are you.

> "Little children (believers, dear ones), you are of God, and you belong to Him and have [already] overcome them [the agents of the antichrist]; because He who is in you is greater than he (Satan) who is in the world [of sinful mankind]."
>
> −1 John 4:4 *AMP*

62

Thoughts, oh, thoughts. They try and consume. Thoughts, oh, thoughts. I can't control you on my own. Thoughts, you come and roam. I dig deep into the spirit and say, rebuke them out and watch me pray. I will take these thoughts captive and say, I know your word saves me from these thoughts' night and day.

"But his delight is in the law of the Lord, and on His law [His precepts and teachings] he [habitually] meditates day and night."

–Psalms 1:2 *AMP*

The footsteps of Jesus. Oh, how I love to walk in the footsteps of Jesus. So bold, so fearless, so kind. Never would he back down but always would pray and walk through, walk forward, walk on. Oh, how I love to walk in the footsteps of Jesus. When trials, tests and temptations come, I know I can be so strong. When my mind and heart is set from above, I know these footsteps would never steer me wrong. Oh, how I love to walk in the footsteps of Jesus. These footsteps guide me, lead me, comfort me and give me peace. Thank you, Jesus, for walking with me.

> *"For [as a believer] you have been called for this purpose, since Christ suffered for you, leaving you an example, so that you may follow in His footsteps."*
>
> −1 Peter 2:21 *AMP*

64

Walk with me and talk with me, so I shall never miss, never miss this life you came to give. Help me, Father. Help me see when I fall and feel defeat. Help me step into your glory and see that all that was meant to harm could never be. You are in control and always see. Father, oh, Father, you are always there. Father, oh, Father, how you care. Father, oh, Father, it's you I shall share all my love and cast my cares.

> "Protect me from harm; keep an eye on me as you would a child who is reflected in the twinkling of your eye. Yes, hide me within the shelter of your embrace, under your outstretched wings."
>
> —Psalms 17:8 *TPT*

Father, you tell us we are yours. Father, you show us we are to be held by the king of kings, by his glory. We will rise and never fail, Father. This is the story I shall tell when life gets hard, and people come against. Help me remember this was a part of your plan, for me to believe, to conquer my worst enemies. Help me, Father, to see, to receive your peace and joy in everything, in your suffering. These persecutions shall ease. You paid them all and I will never doubt, for I have a king, a king, a risen resurrection, glorified king.

> "On his robe and on his thigh, he had inscribed a name: King of Kings and Lord of Lords."
>
> —Revelation 19:16 *TPT*

66

Never will I miss. Never will I leave. Never will I walk this road lonely, for I always have a helper, a friend, a Father, so dear. I shall never walk this life in fear when enemies come against and try to take me out with their hits. Help me remember who lives inside me. That is a battle already won and I hold the authority.

> "And they were astonished at His teaching,
> for His word was with authority."
> –Luke 4:32 NKJV

Your love shines bright. Your love is my delight. All I ask, all I seek at the end of the day, it's just you and me. Let me never forget this love nailed to a tree. This price that was paid to live fully. A life abundant and free. A life with wisdom and peace. Oh, this life I shall never forget. The day you went to the cross and never looked with regret.

"But God demonstrates His own love toward us, in that while we were still sinners, Christ died for us."

–Romans 5:8 *NKJV*

68

Oh, how I love to hear you say, oh how I love to see you pray in all confidence, love and truth, in all your devotion it's true. Oh, how I love to hear you say, go now child all is okay. Let go and let me be the only one you seek. Go now child hear me say, you have gone and done all these things. I say go now in peace, go now loving me. One day you will see this life you gave for me will be heaven and victory.

> "Nevertheless, do not rejoice at this, that the spirits are subject to you, but rejoice that your names are recorded in heaven."
>
> —Luke 10:20 *AMP*

Hits, kicks and bites all come and hit you from out of sight. Soar, conquer, win and grin when I walk with you. How can I not win? Shallow talk and sweet revenge, that's for the lost that's went astray, and you have called me to overcome my enemies with sweet words of praise. You have called me to win and not live in defeat from the evil one's schemes.

> "To the weak I became [as the] weak, to win the weak. I have become all things to all men, so that I may by all means [in any and every way] save some [by leading them to faith in Jesus Christ]."
> —1 Corinthians 9:22 *AMP*

70

I love you, Lord, it's true. I love the good days, bad days and less than days too, because I know these days come with truth. I love you, Lord, oh, it's true. I love your word, your smile, your love, it's true. I love the way you teach, it's true. It's our way to know and honor you. I love you, Lord, it's true. I love that I'm your child and nothing changes that, it's true. I love you, Lord, forgive me of my sins. I would rather die to myself than live in sin.

"But you, Timothy, are a man of God; so, run from all these evil things. Pursue righteousness and a godly life, along with faith, love, perseverance, and gentleness."

—1 Timothy 6:11 *NLT*

All these battles. All these fights compares to nothing you endured that Friday night. Help me forgive. Help me see this battle we face; you hold the victory. Help me see. Help me see, oh, Father with your eyes to see. Help me see. Help me see with your eyes and heart to love my enemies. Help me, Father, help me, to see how you forgave when nailed to that tree. Help me, Father, help me see the only thing that matters is you died to save me.

> *"But he was pierced for our rebellion, crushed for our sins. He was beaten so we could be whole. He was whipped so we could be healed."*
>
> —Isaiah 53:5 *NLT*

72

All these twists, turns and wrong roads has led me to find my only hope. My only hope is in you not this world, people or lies, it's true. My only hope comes deep within. I can look up and see it's you and I win. My only hope is you, it's true. My only hope, my devotion, my everything points to you.

"Remember your promise to me; it is my only hope."

—Psalms 119:49 *NLT*

When your friends, family and hometown turned against, how did you let go and move on without them? It's hard. It's hard. It's so hard to see, mostly because I don't understand how they could treat you so bad. How they couldn't believe you were sent from above. How they couldn't see you were so much love. How they couldn't see those signs, miracles, wonders and that tree boggles my mind. Boggles me. Help me, Father, when the same come against me. Help me, Father, to let go and repent. Help me, Father, for one day I know I will be living in heaven with your hand to hold.

> "And they took offense at him. But Jesus said to them, "A prophet is not without honor except in his hometown and in his own household."
>
> –Matthew 13:57 *ESV*

74

Sometimes I want to scream from insecurity. Sometimes I want to shout from the nonsense that dwells within. Sometimes I want to punch out all the lies that circle around in my head. Sometimes I want to run and not forgive. Sometimes I want to kick the doors down. Sometimes I want to fly off the handle in a crowd. Sometimes I would love to repay evil with a sin when I know in my heart this is no way to live. I have an enemy that loves to come and take my knees, so I can't think to pray. I have an enemy that loves to steal my peace, that makes me believe lies that are unseen. I have an enemy that loves to cause despair. Oh, how I can feel him sometimes, so bare. I have an enemy that knows he can fight but cannot win because I have a God stronger than any of this.

> *"What causes quarrels and what causes fights among you? Is it not this, that your passions are at war within you?"*
>
> –James 4:1 *ESV*

Y ou say to let go and look above. You say to let go and simply love. You say to let go so I can be free. You say to let go but sometimes it isn't easy. You say to let go of pride and deceit. You say to let go and live, just believe. You say to let go child, you win. You say to let go and run with a grin. Letting go is hard to do. Letting go means I have to trust fully in you. Letting go. Oh, how I would love to see letting go be easier. Letting go of past hurts and pain. Letting go and being changed. Letting go you tell us to do. Letting go means finding you.

"And 'don't sin by letting anger control you.' Don't let the sun go down while you are still angry."

—Ephesians 4:26 *NLT*

Trust. Trust. I trust in you. Trust is so easy but hard to do. When tough times come, and my trust wavers undone. Help me focus and repent. Help me find my trust in you again.

> "Trust in the Lord with all your heart; do not depend on your own understanding."
>
> —Proverbs 3:5 *NLT*

Hope, sacrifice, love and truth. All these good things, he has done for you. All these good things, we take for granted and know. All these good things that always flow from the heart of our loving Father. It's true, he died to love you. Father, help me see, you gave up your life for me to be free.

> *"For freedom Christ has set us free; stand firm therefore, and do not submit again to a yoke of slavery."*
>
> –Galatians 5:1 *ESV*

78

When does all this war stop? All this hate. When do we stop and praise your name? When do we stop fighting other men? When do we stop and love them? When do we stop hate and war? Father, I know your heart breaks at these roars, these attacks on others too, when do we stop and praise you? Father, help this world see when we hate one another we are hating thee. Father, stopping this is my heart's cry. Stop these evil lies. Father, stop this awful life where we put ourselves above and fight. Father, help us see when we give up our life for yours to keep, we will love you and all our enemies

"But anyone who does not love does not know God, for God is love."

−1 John 4:8 *NLT*

Father, I come to you. I need rest. I can't lay another burden on my chest. I need you, Father, now more than ever. It's true. I need you, Father, to sweep in and rescue me. It's true. I need you, Father, these cares are too much. I need you, Father, you are my only love, I need you, Father, please help me see that when I walk through all these insecurities, you walk with me. I need you, Father. I repent. I need you, Father. I have sinned. I need you, Father. My eyes can see that when I surrender and seek, Thee, my worries fall at your feet. Father, oh, Father, I come again. Father, oh, Father, I have seen these men come to tear your name apart. Come, Father. Help. I need you now more than ever for sure. I can't fight this fight alone. You have called me to be still and know this battle is won, and I'm no longer in defeat. This battle is yours and not mine to keep.

"Be still and know that I am God! I will be honored by every nation. I will be honored throughout the world."

—Psalms 46:10 *NLT*

80

Lord, I'm tired. I need your rest. Lord, I know you know best. Lord, I'm tired and need your rest. This stress I carry is wearing me down. This stress I carry takes me to the ground. Father, help me let go and release. Help me to have eyes to see, that when I let go and release, you always have the very best for me.

> "Then Jesus said, "Come to me, all of you who are weary and carry heavy burdens, and I will give you rest."
>
> –Matthew 11:28 *NLT*

Sickness you come. Sickness you roar. Sickness you take us down and store all your weight, all your hurt, all your troubles here. You take us at our knees. You take us and make us believe we are in defeat. Oh, but when our eyes stay fixed on Thee, we will see this sickness that comes. This sickness that runs through without stopping or slowing down. We will not bow down to this. We will rest and be blessed. We will not accept this but see healing. A Father that loves to heal. We will see healing. Yes, we will see healing after healing, day by day, with a Father that stays by our side every step of the way. Sickness, you are no good to me. Sickness, you must flee at the mere mention of his name. So run, scream and shout. Jesus died to give us clout, authority over you, leave us alone and run. Flee, now leave us alone. We will win over sickness. We will win, win, win over sickness. Watch us win over sickness. Watch us win. Your timing, Lord, not ours. Your timing, Lord, not ours. We want to see you move and stay in peace until it's through.

"O Lord my God, I cried to you for help, and
you restored my health."

–Psalms 30:2 *NLT*

Word of God. Speak. We ask, Lord, show us even our small tasks. May we obey your loving will. May we lay ours down and not kill. Not kill what you have given us to do. Not kill those dreams. Lord, you choose. Do not kill this love in our hearts. Do not kill when we fall apart. Lord, your will is what we want. Your will is my all and all. May you stretch us but not fall. Lord, you are my everything, it's true, my life. I want to honor you.

"I have not departed from his commands but have treasured his words more than daily food."

—Job 23:12 *NLT*

Lord, it's me. I have been drowning and so weak. Lord, I want to be healed. Lord, I want to feel. I want to feel your touch. I want to know I am loved no matter what may come against. I want to always look up from my sin, repent and say have all of me, Lord, take this away. I know you are a healer. It's true. I know I am healed because of you. Lord, please heal me now. I can't go another minute longer without knowing how, when or why this is. Show me, Lord, show me your loving kindness from within.

> *"Confess your sins to each other and pray for each other so that you may be healed. The earnest prayer of a righteous person has great power and produces wonderful results."*
>
> –James 5:16 *NLT*

84

Where do truth and lies come from? Truth comes from you. Lies come from evil. It's true. All his evil schemes and disguise. Oh, how he loves to lie. Father, I repent. When I have sinned, I repent. Allowing him to enter in these thoughts in my mind takes my cares and throws them deeper everywhere. Lord, I repent. I know the truth you have sent. Help me when I stumble and fall. Help me when I don't call. Don't call upon you Lord to stand up and stand firm, for without you, I feel so poor. Without you these lies rage like a storm.

"Save me! Rescue me from the power of my enemies. Their mouths are full of lies; they swear to tell the truth, but they lie instead."

—Psalms 144:11 *NLT*

The angels you give. The angels we receive to help us along, not just in our dreams. These angels are for love, protection and guidance, too. These angels we have are so very true.

> *"Then an angel from heaven appeared*
> *and strengthened him."*
>
> –Luke 22:43 *NLT*

86

These written letters, Lord. You say these written letters, Lord, we shall obey. Thank you for your words in print. Thank you for dying and rising again. I could not imagine living without this hope. I could not imagine this was all for show. Father, thank you for sending him to save us all from our ugly sins.

> *"Jesus told him, 'I am the way, the truth, and the life. No one can come to the Father, except through me.'"*
>
> —John 14:6 *NLT*

I repent. I repent. I say, go lay down all your burdens and do not stray. I repent. I repent. It is the faith and love from my Father that keeps me grounded. I repent. I repent of pride, for pride leads to destruction and so many lies. I repent. I repent. It's true. I repent and choose to honor and love you.

> *"Repent, for the kingdom of heaven is at hand."*
> —Matthew 3:2 *ESV*

88

You have called us to love. You have called us to let go. When we let go, we have power to hold. Power to hold onto what is really yours. To control the power, the power, the power to let go.

> "But he said to me, "My grace is sufficient for you, for my power is made perfect in weakness." Therefore, I will boast all the more gladly of my weaknesses, so that the power of Christ may rest upon me."
>
> –2 Corinthians 12:9 *ESV*

We are free. We are free. We are so abundantly free. To walk free is to be all with him. To walk free is to lay down our what could have been. To walk free is to be holy with Thee. To walk free is my choice to live with Thee and see. To be free is really to be free from me.

"So, if the Son sets you free, you will be free indeed."
—John 8:36 *ESV*

90

Running ragged. Running scared. Running through all your cares. Running afraid. Running deep. Running is something I don't want to keep running from you. Running with truth is where I want to be. The only running I can do in victory.

> "Yet in all these things we are more than conquerors
> and gain an overwhelming victory through Him who
> loved us [so much that He died for us]."
>
> –Romans 8:37 *AMP*

All these dark cries. All these hurts. Tell me, Father, where is their worth? Where do they put their value at? Where, oh, where, Father, can they say they are had? Look down and give them mercy, for they do not know. Look down and say, child, I am here to hold. Look down on the pitiful and rebuke what they see. Look down, Father, and love them as you love me.

> *"It is because of the Lord's loving kindnesses that we are not consumed, Because His [tender] compassions never fail."*
>
> –Lamentations 3:22 *AMP*

92

You say we will suffer here on this earth. You say you give us strength to suffer even more. You say this suffering will one day be no more. Lord, when we suffer, may we know how you suffered more.

> "For I consider [from the standpoint of faith] that the sufferings of the present life are not worthy to be compared with the glory that is about to be revealed to us and in us!"
>
> —Romans 8:18 *AMP*

Oh, the miracles you have seen. Oh, the miracles you have decreed. Oh, the miracles in a sense. It's a miracle for you to love all men, even when they choose to lie and backstab you. Even though they persecuted and beat you, Father, how did you love? When they spit on you, how did you forgive? So true. Teach me, show me your heart, Father. This is my part to heal, when others rip me apart.

> "While they were nailing Jesus to the cross, he prayed
> over and over, 'Father, forgive them, for they don't
> know what they're doing.' The soldiers, after they
> crucified him, gambled over his clothing."
>
> —Luke 23:34 *TPT*

94

That cross you bore for our sins to be no more. That cross you bore to free us forevermore. That cross you bore forever, we shall roar into the kingdom come, thy will be done. Your kingdom, we see a kingdom on our knees. Thank you, Jesus, for dying to set us free, to receive eternity.

"I am crucified with Christ: nevertheless, I live; yet not I, but Christ liveth in me: and the life which I now live in the flesh I live by the faith of the Son of God, who loved me, and gave himself for me."

–Galatians 2:20 *KJV*

Miracles. We see miracles. We believe miracles. We sense miracles. We praise him. Miracles of truth. Miracles. Believe they are true miracles. You are miracles. Never too far miracles. We see miracles. We believe, Jesus, miracles are your thing to protect us from all things.

"And God hath both raised up the Lord and will also raise up us by his own power."

−1 Corinthians 6:14 *KJV*

96

Persecution at your name. Persecution has a loud ring. Persecution is intense. Persecution comes against. Persecution is rarely found from a man wearing a crown. Persecution, I have seen you. Persecution looks ugly too. Persecution is found. Persecution has made its round. Persecution, one thing I know, you have no real hold. Jesus was persecuted, so I can suffer persecution too. Persecution, one day I won't find you when I'm in heaven, praising him. It's true.

> *"Yes, and all who desire to live godly in*
> *Christ Jesus will suffer persecution."*
> –II Timothy 3:12 *NKJV*

The knocks, hits, settle blows, they come again and forever more. They come and hit again and again. They come just when I feel like giving in. I take a deep breath and say, I don't care and here comes another snare. From what I know from all these blows is that I have a God that loves to hold all my worries, all my cares, all my stress and feelings of despair. So, when these hits come and never stop, I look up and hear, child, I have already paid for these, rest it was bought.

"You were bought at a price; do not become slaves of men."

–I Corinthians 7:23 *NKJV*

98

The kicks, I hear him say. These kicks will be gone one day. These kicks. I hear him be. These kicks are from the enemy. These kicks won't be here for long. These kicks will make you strong. These kicks, I know they hurt you. These kicks can't take you down or turn you around. They can make you strong all day long. Cast him out and pour a long praise of my name. These kicks are nothing for my name.

> *"And Jesus answered and said to him, 'Get behind Me, Satan! For it is written, 'You shall worship the Lord your God, and Him only you shall serve.'"*
>
> –Luke 4:8 *NKJV*

Sick and all alone, let me hear you say you are on your throne. When I'm sick and nowhere to turn, let me feel you even more. When I'm sick and feel like giving up, let me see you pour from your cup. Healer, oh, healing, I ask. I know you can heal. It's no small task. You can heal in a second, it's true. You can heal in a thought, why don't you? Lord, help me to see it's your time, not mine. Help me to wait and be fine. Help me to sit and see that your time is the best time for me.

> *"O Lord, if you heal me, I will be truly healed; if you save me, I will be truly saved. My praises are for you alone!"*
>
> –Jeremiah 17:14 *NLT*

100

They say it's Good Friday, but Jesus, how did you feel with all your pain? How did you feel with the betrayal and the ones that didn't come? Oh, Jesus, how did you feel when all this came undone? How did you feel being whipped and beat? How did you feel? Did you feel defeat? How did you feel when they mocked and spit on you? Oh, Jesus, how did you feel with no one loving you? You came, you taught and now our sins are bought. On Good Friday, I would have to say it was a very good day. You have conquered that grave and forevermore we shall praise your glorious name. Jesus, today I thank you for the cross. I thank you, Jesus, for what you endured for us, to be complete in the cross. Your love shown best, your love for us while we were still in sin. Thank you for the cross. Thank you for enduring all that pain, for now we all have a new name.

Thank you for the cross.

So, so, so grateful for the agony you bore for our sins. To be no more. I don't get how someone could love this much. I don't get how a Father could send and give up his only son for me. Father, help my eyes and heart to see this precious gift given from Thee. This precious gift. Help me see that only a father's love could take this on and forever be strong through life and the battles ahead. Help me to lift my head and see all this was paid on Calvary for me to be free.

We are free by the blood of Jesus.

102

Father, you are so sure. Your heart is so pure. The love that was sent. The love that has always been. Father, you are so good. You take me through the dark and tell me not to fall apart. This love, Father, is true and every day I shall honor you with the love you have given me. Father, oh, Father, help me to see and believe you always hold the highest victories.

> "... saying, 'Is this the one who trusted in God? Now let's see if Yahweh will come to your rescue! Let's see how much he delights in him!'"
>
> –Psalms 22:8 *TPT*

I run to the Father. I run past what this world offers, and I run to my loving Father that forgives of these grueling sins. I run to him to be free. I run to him to see this sin has no hold on me. This sin must flee. This sin is gone away. Oh, how I love to say, Lord, my Father, Jesus, my one. This has been bought and all done. Your plans for me will prevail when I repent and do. You will, Father, keep me holy and safe. Keep me in your arms until that sweet, sweet day.

> *"But if we freely admit our sins when his light uncovers them, he will be faithful to forgive us every time. God is just to forgive us our sins because of Christ, and he will continue to cleanse us from all unrighteousness."*
>
> —1 John 1:9 *TPT*

104

You rose from the dead. You conquered that grave, rolled that stone away. How could this be? What a miracle to see. Jesus, you are Thee. You are our one and only. Thank you, Father, for eyes to see. Thank you for our helper to receive this blessing. Father, oh, Father, that grave couldn't hold you down. Father, oh, Father, that crown of thorns, those nails went deep. All this, Father, for our souls to forever be. Thank you for this act I never seen. Thank you for this, now, we shall forever be together in eternity.

He is risen hallelujah.

Where does our hope come from, our fight, our strife? Where do the troubles go and take us behind? Where does truth come from? Is it hit or miss? No, not with our helper to guide us and never miss. Where do these hits, punches, scratches you see come from? It hits me in the dark where I cannot see. Where does this pain and suffering dwell? Why don't we all praise Him? This is the story I shall tell, Father, when I'm falling, worn and weak, pick me up and help me speak life, oh life and healing comes you see when you dare to believe and speak into your disbelief.

> *"Nothing is more appealing than speaking beautiful, life-giving words. For they release sweetness to our souls and inner healing to our spirits."*
>
> –Proverbs 16:24 *TPT*

106

You walked. You talked. You teached. You preached. How did you feel when they left you on those streets? How did you feel when they mocked and told lies? How did you feel when they hit you between the eyes? How did you feel through all of this? How did you feel, Father? Were you crushed by this? How did you feel when the lost were found? How did you feel when you wore the crown? How did you feel choosing his will? How did you feel taking on our sins? Even when you knew someone would not love and come for you, some would say you weren't truth. How do you love and forgive these men? Father, oh, father, show me how to forgive and love like this.

> *"Teach me more about you, how you work and how you move, so that I can walk onward in your truth until everything within me brings honor to your name."*
>
> —Psalms 86:11 *TPT*

The rumbles and shakes. All the tornados and earthquakes. The trials, tests and tribulations we face. Never will we endure more than you did that day. Never will we face the death you gave for us to see life in a whole new way.

> *"And by his one perfect sacrifice he made us perfectly holy and complete for all time!"*
>
> –Hebrews 10:14 *TPT*

108

Pushed and shoved. Father, you knew this love hits and spits. You faced all of it. Torn, tried and true. You always did what you were put to do. Overcoming sin. You never were guilty of this. Strong and humble. Love that rumbles. You shook that grave and walked out to lay a road less paved. Some will choose to walk with you. Some will choose another way and lose. Help me to always stay in your will, in your faith, Father. Oh, Father, shall I never be one that strays but chooses to obey.

> *"... he humbled himself in obedience to God and died a criminal's death on a cross."*
>
> –Philippians 2:8 *NLT*

Father, my heart is yours. Father, take it, have it, make it pure. Father, you are my true delight. Father, you always put up a fight for me to win, to have peace and grin for me, to love. Oh, Father, it's what my heart longs for. For me to forgive, to let go, see and repent. Examine my heart. It was always yours from the start.

> "The sacrifice you desire is a broken spirit. You will not reject a broken and repentant heart, O God."
>
> —Psalms 51:17 *NLT*

110

Let go. Release. Let go and be. Let go and see. He holds the highest victories. Let go and see. Let go and be. When we let go, we truly see the Father at work. The Father knows our worth. He holds all the keys. Oh, child, he says let go and watch me.

"Seek his will in all you do, and he will show you which path to take."

—Proverbs 3:6 *NLT*

My children. They are a precious gift. My children. I sure adore them. My children. My hearts delight. My children. Be still and do not fight. This world is tough and will try and come against, but you have Jesus and that you are heaven sent. It's true, my children, Jesus gave me you. My children. You are so very true. When I count my blessings, I count you twice. You are a mother's pure delight.

Thank you, Jesus, for my precious children.

112

It's dark. I have seen very dark days. I wonder. Where did they come from and why have they stayed? I looked up and seen you conquer that grave and remember this darkness simply can't stay when I set my mind above and pray, pray, pray.

> *"He led them from the darkness and deepest gloom;*
> *he snapped their chains."*
>
> —Psalms 107:14 *NLT*

Through the hills and valleys, you were good. Through the sickness and depression, you were good. Through the panic attacks and sleepless nights, you were so good. You held me, never let go and pushed me through. Through my children's birth, you were good. Through my wedding day and first years, you were good. Through the ups and downs, battles and defeats, the mountain tops and grave sides, you never left me. For I know you are always good, and you have helped me from where I stood from the deepest of sorrow to the most joy I have ever felt. Lord Jesus, Holy Spirit, you were always there and dealt.

> "And we know that God causes everything to work together for the good of those who love God and are called according to his purpose for them."
>
> –Romans 8:28 *NLT*

114

You have never left my side, not even the darkest nights, not in the fear and anxiety. No, you crushed all those insecurities. Forever, I am grateful. Can't you see, I owe you my life and you gave me eternity.

"Always be joyful."
−1 Thessalonians 5:16 *NLT*

In the deep, deep parts of my soul. In the deep parts, I don't want to go. In the deep parts, you search and see. In the deep, is where you will be. In the deep, I see you there. In the deep, I cast all my cares. In the deep, Father, never leave, for in the deep, I know you love me.

> *"Such amazing mysteries are found within every miracle that nearly everyone seems to miss. Those with no discernment can never really discover the deep and glorious secrets hidden in your ways."*
>
> –Psalms 92:6 *TPT*

116

Father, how many times shall we count the cost? How many times shall I follow until I never get lost? How many times shall I sin? How many times shall you forgive? Father, help us see that you died to set us free. Father, for I know eternity is where I will be, because you died loving me.

> "Lord and Master, I am your loving servant,
> and now I can die content, for you have fulfilled
> your promise to me. With my own eyes I have
> seen your Word, the Savior you sent into the world."

–Luke 2:29-31 *TPT*

Holy Ghost, you are a friend of mine. Holy Ghost, the very best and so fine. Holy Ghost, never leave, for I could not live without you in me. Holy Ghost, an honor, it's true, to house a home just for you. May I die to self for you to live in a place you call me your friend. Holy Ghost, you are all I need. Holy Ghost, you awaken me. Holy Ghost, you are welcome here. Holy Ghost, you cry my tears. Holy Ghost, never leave, for I will never be who I am without you. Thank you for giving me truth.

> *"May you never reject me! May you never take from me your sacred Spirit!"*
>
> —Psalms 51:11 *TPT*

118

Like a rushing wind blowing through my peace. I leave with you. So holy. So good. This fruit I leave you to bear, share it everywhere. With my spirit I pour out, child, you never have to doubt.

> "So, letting your sinful nature control your mind leads to death. But letting the Spirit control your mind leads to life and peace."
>
> –Romans 8:6 *NLT*

Father, Father, forgive me for I have sinned. Father, Father, oh, how I repent. The joy, strength, struggles, too. I give you, my life. I shall not lose with you.

> "You will find true success when you find me, for I have insight into wise plans that are designed just for you. I hold in my hands living, understanding, courage, and strength."
>
> —Proverbs 8:14 *TPT*

120

The world has fallen into the pits of hell. The world has stopped ringing your bell. Politics, religion too, all this fake news. Father, awaken us to see that you are the one that holds the keys. Father, awaken us to see life is not made to be as we see. As we see with our eyes. This is not our Fathers desires. Father, awaken the world to see, it's only you we shall see.

"What bliss you experience when your heart is pure!
For then your eyes will open to see more and more of
God."

–Matthew 5:8 *TPT*

You gave us words. You gave us life. You gave us precious time. May we use these gifts you have given us to be a light to the world of heaven's armies. May we sit and never miss, what you gave with a kiss. May we sit and never miss, what you gave with a kiss. The betrayal that took place all those years ago, what was at stake, Father, that kiss he gave you. That kiss was so true. The betrayal from that day has led us here to pray. To pray. Never to be the one that would betray and leave you. To be undone. For as we know, you mean more than a show. For as we see, we believe heavens armies.

"Jesus looked at him with sorrow and said, 'A kiss, Judas? Are you really going to betray the Son of Man with a kiss?'"

–Luke 22:48 *TPT*

Open doors. Shut the doors. Open doors. Shut the doors.
You open and shut. You open and shut our eyes, our heart. You
open and shut our life, our call, our will, our desires. You open
and shut. You open and shut. You open and shut. May we see
the open and shut as grace. To believe the open and shut is you
loving thee.

> "Write the following to the messenger of the
> congregation in Philadelphia, for these are the solemn
> words of the Holy One, the true one, who has David's
> key, who opens doors that none can shut and who
> closes doors that none can open: I know all that you've
> done. Now I have set before you a wide-open door that
> none can shut. For I know that you possess only a little
> power, yet you've kept my word and haven't denied my
> name."
>
> –Revelation 3:7-8 TPT

Windows we see. Windows are glass. Windows we ask. The windows of our soul, do you look upon and see us glow? Do you look in, to see heaven's glory shining upon thee? Do you look in to see everything you made us to be? These windows you see, these windows built to dream. Look out those windows and believe you have everything you meant to dream.

We are open vessels, look in to see we honor the king of kings.

Provider of our health. Provider of our wealth. Provider of our soul. Provider of our know. Provider of our truth. Provider of our shoes. Our shoes of peace. May we walk along side, Thee, carrying the weight of our sin. No, you have called us to repent. To change the way we think. To stop, listen and obey. Provider of all my days. I will honor you and say you are my provider. Never shall I take. You are the key to heaven's gates.

*"We acknowledge you as our Provider
of all we need each day."*

—Matthew 6:11 *TPT*

The keys you hold. The keys you throw. The keys of grace. The keys of strength. The keys to unlock all life's takes. The keys to dream. The keys to believe. The keys of faith. The keys to take. You hold them in your hand and unlock our daily plans. You hold them in your hand and unlock our daily plans. May we never miss. May we never arise without you. May we never think we could choose anything but you, Father. Help me always see you.

> *"May we never forget that Yahweh works wonders for every one of his devoted lovers. And this is how I know that he will answer my every prayer."*
>
> —Psalms 4:3 *TPT*

126

Your will be done, Father. Your will be done. Your will be done. Your will is our will. We can let go and see. You hold the victory, and we shall be free.

"Your kingdom come. Your will be done on earth as it is in heaven."

–Matthew 6:10 *NKJV*

You are holy. You are sure. You are everything. So pure. You came to give life and not death. Father, you ask us to live like there is nothing left. Father, you died for us to live. You came and took on sin. Help us to see in our unbelief. Help us to trust you with everything. Father, my only prayer is to seek you forever and ever for eternity.

> *"... but as He who called you is holy you also be holy in all your conduct."*
>
> —I Peter 1:15 *NKJV*

128

You came for us. For one, just one, to know you. We are loved. We are loved and full of grace. You send down and call us by name. Oh, never were we a mistake. Never shall our past keep us at bay. We know to repent and say, Father, forgive me. You have paid for all of this. I just cry out to you, to please forgive and help me change my ways. Father, oh, Father, this I shall pray.

> *"I correct and discipline everyone I love. So be diligent and turn from your indifference."*
>
> –Revelation 3:19 *NLT*

You are the way, the truth, the life. All else I will cast aside. To surrender and let go. To know and hold. The only thing that matters to me is to listen as you speak. To obey in the hard things and walk in the uncertainty, for I know wherever you lead, I will always be in the arms and peace of my, Father, loving me.

> *"Even though Jesus was God's Son, he learned obedience from the things he suffered."*
>
> –Hebrews 5:8 *NLT*

130

You tell us to walk. You tell us to share. You tell us to love one another without fault, without sin. How did you do this, Jesus? How did you grin when others came against? How did you smile and walk on? How did you preach to those who were wrong? How did you love so much? How did you forgive and not hold all those punches, hits and cuts? How did you? Oh, how did you? I will never know how you walked this earth and never sinned. You are my true champion.

> "For God made Christ, who never sinned, to be the offering for our sin, so that we could be made right with God through Christ."
>
> –2 Corinthians 5:21 *NLT*

You take us by the hand and say come, child. Do not be afraid. I will take you and send you through. Don't fear. You will never lose. Child, oh, be still. I will fill you with peace and never leave. I will hold you for eternity. Death you will not see. Heaven is your home. This, you will reap, as you only believe in me.

> *"You will keep him in perfect peace, whose mind is stayed on You, because he trusts in You."*
>
> —Isaiah 26:3 *NKJV*

132

Souls you save. Souls you keep. Souls like mine. We love to reap all your goodness, all you share. Jesus, Holy Spirit, you are welcome here. Come, Holy Spirit, flood through me. Pour your cup over me. Jesus, I look up and see only your goodness and everlasting glory.

> "So, Jesus taught them this prayer: "Our heavenly Father, may the glory of your name be the center on which our life turns. May your Holy Spirit come upon us and cleanse us. Manifest your kingdom on earth."
>
> –Luke 11:2 *TPT*

Water, water, water, holy water. So pure. Dive in. There is nothing like it. I'm sure. Holy water, you are so clear. Holy water, I love when you are near. I dive right in. Washed and clean. Wipe away all my insecurities. Defeat is gone. Living is here. Your holy water is all I feel.

Be washed by the water holy and cleansed.

134

Father, you say you give and take away when our eyes can't see the right way. Help us look up and say you know best, and I may never understand but you will. Father, your plan is all I seek. Help me believe you always have the best and see with eyes of eternity.

"And see if there is any wicked way in me. And lead me in the way everlasting."

–Psalms 139:24 *NKJV*

You came to save the lost. You came to seek what never could've been unless you walked out his plan. Jesus, we owe you our lives. Let's count the cost and never die without showing you our faith and taking on your name. Help us to stay, never leave and always obey for we know this life will be no more one day. We will be living with our saving grace.

"For the Son of Man came to seek and save those who are lost."

–Luke 19:10 *NLT*

136

Lord, I look up to you and see the light. I look up and know all is alright. I look up and the peace floods me. I look up and my eyes only see glory. I look up and wonder. I look up and gaze. Father, how did you leave that place? Place to send a son to save us that are lost. How did you pay the price that no other could've bought? Father, you are a mystery to me. A mystery that I love to believe. One sweet day, Father, I yearn to hear you say, child come home with me with to stay.

"For then you will have your delight in the Almighty and lift up your face to God."

–Job 22:26 NKJV

As I sit here and think, as I sit here and dream, I look back and remember all those things you spoke. All those things you foretold. I never knew then, what I know now. I never knew just how much You could wow, wow, wow. As I sit here tonight, all I can see is your delight, your joy, your victory. You speaking over me child. You did it. You won. Now, let's go along as I have more work for you here to do. Live this life in truth. Obey and love and praise. All this will bring you home to me one day.

> *"I press toward the goal for the prize of the upward call of God in Christ Jesus."*
> –Philippians 3:14 *NKJV*

138

Oh, the excitement and joy it brings when you take your hand and bless me. Oh, Father, I love to see your hand. I love to hear and follow your plan. Help me, Father, to walk in your ways. Help me, Father, to always stop, listen and obey. I have lived my way long enough and my way doesn't fill this cup. Help me to stop and remember it's all you. Help me to stop and glorify truth. You are the Father of all good things. You are the Father that loves to hear your children say thank you. Father, for you are so good to me. Thank you, Father, it's only You I shall seek.

"Help me, O Lord my God! Oh, save me according to Your mercy,"

—Psalms 109:26 NKJV

Where does the chaos and confusion come from? One minute I'm walking in peace, the next, there is a war raging inside me. Help me, Father, stand up against. Help me, Father, cast it out and repent. I will not conform to the patterns of this world, but I will bow down to You and truly soar.

"Where do wars and fights come from among you? Do they not come from your desires for pleasure that war in your members?"

–James 4:1 *NKJV*

140

This faith, this faith and what it has taken to get me here. This faith, this faith moved mountains into the cold air. This faith, this faith is everything to me. It helped me grow and open my eyes to see that with faith, anything is possible. It's true, with faith I can believe You will see me through.

> *"But without faith it is impossible to please Him, for he who comes to God must believe that He is, and that He is a rewarder of those who diligently seek Him."*
>
> –Hebrews 11:6 *NKJV*

You give and take away, but you only take what we don't need. You give in abundance. I see. I thank you, Father, for you know best. Next time you take, help me remember it's all for my good, not ever for bad. It's always for my good and when you give, help me see you are the most loving Father given to thee. For this I will forever be thankful, Father, help me not to ever miss your gifts.

> *"Then I will give them one heart, and I will put a new spirit within them, and take the stony heart out of their flesh and give them a heart of flesh,"*
> —Ezekiel 11:19 *NKJV*

142

I will obey. I will sacrifice. I will please you even when it's hard. I will look up and say, Lord, you always know the best way. Help me surrender my flesh, ways, bow down, honor you and pray your way is higher than mine. Your thoughts I can't even contain, Lord, when the trials come, and flesh and spirit are at war; break it and help me roar.

"I delight to do Your will, O my God,
and Your law is within my heart."

—Psalms 40:8 *NKJV*

All this time I spent, all this time wondering. When all this time that passed, I remember I would ask, but when Lord, when will I see? When, Lord, help me believe then that day came and now I can only see your face. Everything you spoke came true. Now I will continue to live and honor you. Help me see past this world. Help me care forevermore that the kingdom of heaven is at hand. Make this all part of my plan. Weed anything not of you out. Set me up and see me out, for I know I could never do this alone. Lord, help me further along.

> *"And I want you to know, my dear brothers and sisters, that everything that has happened to me here has helped to spread the Good News."*
>
> –Philippians 1:12 *NLT*

144

Sickness comes on us thick. Sickness comes and I repent. Lord, help me see a way out. Help, when I can't help myself. I know the tools; you have told me many times. Help me pick back up and rewind back to those days you told me to exercise, eat of health. This world will not bring wealth. Help me, Father, change my ways, for I know this sickness cannot stay.

> *"Don't you remember that when I was with you,*
> *I went over all these things?"*
>
> –2 Thessalonians 2:5 *TPT*

All these thoughts and to-do's. All these things that fill you. All this stuff that comes within. Father, oh, Father, help me rid of them. I need your hand. I need your help. I need you to come in and give me health. This I know, this I ask, Father, oh, Father, please come fast. I need you more. I need you now. Please, help me, Father, in my bow.

> *"... for God bought you with a high price. So, you must honor God with your body."*
>
> —1 Corinthians 6:20 *NLT*

146

As I look at my husband and children you have given me, help me, Father. Help me lead and raise them up right. Help me love them and never fight. As I know they are yours and this I ask, Father, bless them and give them all you have, for I know if they have you in their heart, they will grow and know that you are the key that heaven holds.

"You go before me and follow me.
You place your hand of blessing on my head."

–Psalms 139:5 *NLT*

The people you give to help us get through, the people you give that honor truth, the people you give to help me see, the people you give bless me for I do not know how I would go about without these people you sent from a cloud. A cloud of hope, a cloud of joy, a cloud of forgiveness for me to enjoy! Thank you, Father, for these people I have, for I don't ever want to forget what has not been asked. Thank you, Father, for my people you have sent to love me through the tough times and wins!

Thank you God for your chosen people.

148

As I sit here and wait to hear you speak, as I sit here quiet as can be, I can't help but remember how it was before. How it was when I would not hear your words. Thank you for bringing me to this place. Thank you for calling out my name. For this time as I sit, this time I shall never lose this. For this time, I know what matters most; without it, I just don't seem to flow.

"Thank God for this gift, too wonderful for words!"
−2 Corinthians 9:15 *NLT*

When you speak, I listen up. When you pour, I open up. I love to hear your heart say, child, all is well, all is okay. I love when you lead me through. I love to listen as you speak truth. Your words are life to me. They are everything. I believe without, I just can't see how life could truly be.

> *"And you will know the truth, and*
> *the truth will set you free."*
>
> –John 8:32 *NLT*

150

Trust me, I hear him say. Trust me, I hear him say. When I lay, I ask Lord, how do I do all of these tasks? How do I go on so strong? How do I go? This road seems so long. Trust me, I hear him say. Trust me and lay your worries at my feet. The cross did not defeat. Trust me, I hear him say. Trust me. Cast your cares, cast your worries and I don't cares. Cast them here. Lay them at my feet. Lay them there. Don't go to sleep without feeling me. I am letting you know, when you cast your cares, your worries, I hold. Trust me now. Rest, lay all those cares. Rest, child, rest.

> *"For the Lord delights in his people;*
> *he crowns the humble with victory."*
>
> **—Psalms 149:4** *NLT*

When will the time come? When will it come? When will everything I have asked for come? When? When I ask? You say it's here, but I don't see and ask. When will we see? When, oh when, how could this be? Father, all your glory, all of your love. Help me go low and rise above. It's your time, I see. It's your time, I know. Help me, Father, help me let go.

> *"If you bow low in God's awesome presence, he will eventually exalt you as you leave the timing in his hands."*
>
> −1 Peter 5:6 *TPT*

Father, I repent. Father, I forgive. Father, I bow down and say it's your life I shall live. Bear my cross, you say. Bear my cross and never stray. To be lukewarm is no game, no game, no game you shall ever want to play. So, Father, help me love, help me forgive, help me not judge the rest of them. Help me love, help me see, Father, oh, Father, you are all I need.

"So then, because you are lukewarm, and neither cold nor hot, I will vomit you out of My mouth."

—Revelation 3:16 *NKJV*

Rest, oh, rest, you call us into a deep satisfying rest. A rest, a rest seems foreign sometimes. A rest, a rest, oh, how I like to rest my mind. Calm the thoughts. Calm the stir. Calm them, Father, so I can rest more. Rest in my soul, rest and know, Father, I shall rest and live in fear no more. Rest is what you have called us to. Rest in knowing you are you. Rest sometimes is hard to do, but rest I know surely honors you.

> *"Simply join your life with mine. Learn my ways and you'll discover that I'm gentle, humble, easy to please. You will find refreshment and rest in me."*
>
> –Matthew 11:29 *TPT*

Glory, honor, and praise takes our worries and turns them into faith. Glory, honor, and praise. I shall forever sing your name. Glory, honor, and praise. You are God and I shall not take glory, honor, and truth. Father, oh, Father, I sure adore you.

> "... singing: 'Amen! Praise and glory, wisdom and thanksgiving, honor, power, and might belong to our God forever and ever! Amen!'"
>
> –Revelation 7:12 *TPT*

Father, you ask us to sit. You say Mary chose to sit. You say she chose best. Father, oh, Father, how do many never pass this test? How could they go and never want to sit with you? Father, how, oh, how could they never hear you? If I went a lifetime and never heard you speak, if I went a day and never seen you in me, this life I live would be nothing to live. Father, I pray all these Martha's never take this life of serving and believing. One day they had it all, but never chose to sit and hear you call.

> *"Mary has discovered the one thing most important by choosing to sit at my feet. She is undistracted, and I won't take this privilege from her."*
>
> –Luke 10:42 *TPT*

156

How did Martha serve? How did Mary sit? How did you say Mary chose the best of it? How in this world I live in most believe it's better to serve than sit with thee? How, oh, how did this world go wrong? How, oh, how did the church build these four walls just to bring everyone in to serve but never to teach them to sit with our dear Lord?

> "The Lord answered her, "Martha, my beloved Martha. Why are you upset and troubled, pulled away by all these many distractions?"
>
> —Luke 10:41 *TPT*

When is enough, enough? When does it stop and when do you call bluff? When is enough, enough? I try to show love. I try to show grace but after a while it keeps slapping me in the face. When is enough? When will they get tired and quit coming after me for loving you, for going after truth, for speaking my heart, from hearing you to start? When will they quit? When will they give up? Father, help me forgive again and never let them determine my faith. Oh, Lord, you are my saving grace.

> "Don't be one who is quick to quarrel, for an argument is hard to stop, and you never know how it will end, so don't even start down that road!"
>
> —Proverbs 17:14 *TPT*

Father, I'm tired and running scared. Father, stop me and show me you care when my mind, thoughts, and will strays from you. The enemy comes and I get confused. Help me not stay long there. Help me to lift my head and not care. For you are my one and only, Lord, for you are the one that calms my storm.

> *"But Jesus reprimanded them.*
> *'Why are you gripped with fear? Where is your faith?'*
> *Then he stood and rebuked the storm, saying, 'Be still!'*
> *And instantly it became perfectly calm."*
>
> —Matthew 8:26 *TPT*

Help me release. Help me let go. Help me to see it's your plans I hold when I get lost, lonely or scared. Help me find my way back to your care. Help me see your glory. Help me know what you have for me is always greater than my eyes could see. Help me to hold your victory, Father, this is the only thing I shall seek.

"But she came and worshiped him, pleading again, 'Lord, help me!'"

–Matthew 15:25 *NLT*

160

When my mind runs reckless and thinks all these things, when my peace is gone and I can no longer breathe, when I get up to see another day, when nothing I speak seems to change, when the enemy comes to taunt your children, you show them a way to hold their ground. That shield of faith, those thorns in your crown, you paid the price and that we see. That when he comes, he can't take from thee. Help us be strong and fight with the word. The sword that no evil can destroy the spirit of truth. Oh, how I love you. I speak and know I have victory with you. Yes, those words will shake. Those words, Jesus, Jesus, Jesus will turn him away. Those words I will forever use to shake the enemy, to flee and lead me to peace.

Jesus, Jesus, Jesus

When the battle is won, when I don't agree and move on, when I get sucked into a pit, when I don't feel like fighting to get out of it, when I choose to believe lies and doubt your truth, when I go on and on and never ask you, all those times I could've missed if I would've gave up my will, my pride and chose to repent all those times. I could've missed if I would've humbled and stayed in repentance.

"I tell you, no; but unless you repent, you will all likewise perish."

–Luke 13:5 *NKJV*

When you speak a word and we don't understand, when we think we know all your plans, help us to remember your time is divine. Help us let go and get rid of our pride. Help us to go low and rise to see that when we follow you, we will always reap.

"Seek his will in all you do, and
he will show you which path to take."

—Proverbs 3:6 *NLT*

When shall I give up control and let you move? When shall I say it's not me but you? When shall I fall and say I'm done trying to figure it all out and not run? Father, slow me down. Stop me in my tracks. Help me to see all that I lack. If you aren't the one that guides me through, if you aren't the one I give my life to, if you aren't the one that rules, I will never live with purpose and love. I will never live from your cup. I will never live to be free. I will only live to be seen. Help me, Father, help me be free. Never again will I live for me.

> "Then Jesus said to his disciples, "If you truly want to follow me, you should at once completely reject and disown your own life. And you must be willing to share my cross and experience it as your own, as you continually surrender to my ways."
>
> –Matthew 16:24 *TPT*

164

When I pray, I lay these burdens down. When I stray and feel proud, all the grace my Father gives, all the grace from the one that died for me to live. All the grace my Father shows. How, oh, how when I sin and don't let go, I will never understand this deep love you have. I will never understand how you chose me to be part of your plan. Until that day I see you face to face, Father, help me to see your loving grace.

> *"For by grace you have been saved through faith, and that not of yourselves; it is the gift of God."*
>
> –Ephesians 2:8 *NKJV*

All these days, all these days that come and go. All these times, I don't even know. When will I choose not to worry or fear? When will I see you so very clear? All these days run together, and I miss all what you have, all that you give. Father, when I go into a deep pit of despair, help me, save me from all my cares. Pull me out and show me you are there.

> "My complaint today is still a bitter one, and
> I try hard not to groan aloud."
>
> –Job 23:2 *NLT*

166

The hour is here. The hour is now. Don't waste another moment being too proud. Let go. Let God. This pride will drag along. It will take you out. Father, please show me when I'm all about the wrong things, the world things, help me see. Shake me. Take me to my knees, for I will never prosper there. I will only fail and never bear the humble nature like you are. Teach me. Show me how you are. How you love the unlovable and the ones that hurt you. Help me forgive and be truth. Help me, Father, to see when I give up my life and only serve thee, this is how I will prosper and glorify thee.

> *"He who covers his sins will not prosper, but whoever confesses and forsakes them will have mercy."*
> –Proverbs 28:13 *NKJV*

Unspoken words. Unspoken truth. All these things we don't do, Father. You have called us to love, called us to share, help us, Father, be your eyes and ears! Never shall we doubt. Never shall we fear, Father. We can do all things knowing you are there.

> *"For as by one man's disobedience many were made sinners, so also by one Man's obedience many will be made righteous."*
>
> –Romans 5:19 *NKJV*

168

Father, we ask for your heart. What's your heart? Forgive us for not asking for your heart. You are our one desire. You are fire. May we never go a day again without asking you a simple question. You gave us a way to speak to you. You gave us a way to hear your truth. Father, your heart is everything to me. Father, your heart forever I shall seek.

"But from there you will seek the Lord, your God, and you will find Him if you seek Him with all your heart and with all your soul."

–Deuteronomy 4:29 *NKJV*

Let go. I hear you say, let go, have peace, and stay. Let go. So easy it seems but letting go is really one of the hardest things. Let go. I hear him say, let go and sing my praise. Let go, child. No longer endure. Let go, child. You are filled with my love to conquer all things. You are worthy and loved. Let go, child, smile, it's done.

> *"By pride comes nothing but strife, but with the well-advised is wisdom."*
>
> –Proverbs 13:10 *NKJV*

170

The heart of the matter. I say get to the heart and all else fades, for when I know the heart is okay, I can drop, move on and sing his praise.

> "The spiritually hungry are always ready to learn more, for their hearts are eager to discover new truths."
> —Proverbs 18:15 *TPT*

All these people here I see. All these people you made to be. All these people if they could see what you have called them to be. The love they would bear if they knew how much you cared. Lord, show the hurting, unloved and lost what was paid on that cross. Oh, how this world would be a better place if they lived with love and not full of hate.

> *"But amazingly, God—so full of compassion—still forgave them. He covered over their sins with his love, refusing to destroy them all. Over and over, he held back his anger, restraining wrath to show them mercy."*
>
> —Psalms 78:38 *TPT*

172

The plans we have for ourselves are quite funny compared to what is dealt. Father, help us to let go, surrender, and see those plans compare nothing to what you have for me.

> "Direct me, Yahweh, throughout my journey so I can experience your plans for my life. Reveal the life paths that are pleasing to you."
>
> —Psalms 25:4 *TPT*

People come to shoot us down. They call themselves Christians, but how? They come after you. They come after me, but oh, the depths they must swing. Father, we can take the heat knowing you are our true defender. Wake them up, shake them scared, make them flee. Give us strength to forgive, like you, Father, that's our faith.

> "Even when your path takes me through the valley of deepest darkness, fear will never conquer me, for you already have! Your authority is my strength and my peace. The comfort of your love takes away my fear. I'll never be lonely, for you are near."
>
> —Psalms 23:4 *TPT*

When something hits you from the dark, something comes at you with a bark. Some fear and anxiety you knew before, crept back in and took you to the floor. Where did you come from fear? Go. You can't stay here. You came, but I am found, and my God will win this final round. So go back to hell where you belong. Leave. I am so strong. Nothing will shoot or take me down. I wear the victor's crown. Jesus give me peace and strength to withstand. Tell me how it all goes through your hands. I have comfort in knowing that my Father has me forever to hold.

"... and the peace of God, which surpasses all understanding, will guard your hearts and minds through Christ Jesus."

–Philippians 4:7 *NKJV*

It's me. It's me. I hear him say, it's me. It's me. Come and pray. I see all your struggles, your hurts, your cares. I see them. Like a glass mirror over here. Go now. Let them all go and let them be. I have come to give you peace. Let them go and receive. Let them go and be with me.

> *"For I consider that the sufferings of this present time are not worthy to be compared with the glory which shall be revealed in us."*
>
> —Romans 8:18 *NKJV*

Lord, when I'm tired and I don't feel like going another step, when my faith is barely hanging on, when the whole world looks grim, when I look and only see sin, when my health fails me, when I'm too tired to see, to see, to see the road ahead, I hear you say child, lift your head. It's all okay. This for your own good. I will build you up and send you out. Child, never doubt my love for you. Never doubt it's true. These trials that come will never be without love. Hold tight and persevere. I'm moving you out with no fear.

> *"Dear brothers and sisters, when troubles of any kind come your way, consider it an opportunity for great joy."*
>
> –James 1:2 *NLT*

Father, I counted the cost. You paid the price. You are my heart's delight with everything I am and everything I do. Help me to always love and glorify you. I thank you, Father, for all you have done. I thank you for this life I live, for you are so generous, loving and kind. A Father to me. The one I find holy and true. How blessed am I to love and know you.

> *"For you were bought at a price; therefore, glorify God in your body and in your spirit, which are God's."*
>
> —1 Corinthians 6:20

ABOUT THE AUTHOR

I believe it's the Father, the Son, and the Holy Ghost, and everything else flows from it. I have an amazing husband, Justin, of fifteen years. I have two precious daughters that make my world go round. Addie, 13 and Liv, 8. We reside in Bourbon, MO and founded True Love Ministries. My heart is to flow from the heart of Jesus and tell the world the relationship with our Father is the most important of all.